Contents

Photo: Bangour Village Hospital Grounds
Kate Gray 2001

Clockwise from top left:
Anne Elliot, Michelle Naismith and Sandra Kinsey
Kate Gray and Jeanette Bell
Michelle Naismith and Sandra Kinsey
Anne Elliot and Jocky

My ... man
of ...

Explorations in collaborative practice

FUSION programme
Published by Artlink and The Fruitmarket Gallery, 2002
In association with the Lothian Hospital Arts Consortium

Foreword

This book stands as a testimony to a remarkable project which succeeded in uniting a wide range of art forms and artists with most of the hospitals in Lothian and with many of their patients.

Few want to be admitted to hospital and therefore it is clearly incumbent upon those responsible for the care of patients to try and make their stay as enjoyable as possible in the circumstances. This seems a self-evident truth, as does the fact that their working environment is important to staff. FUSION has enriched the NHS in Lothian and succeeded in weaving artistic activity into the fabric of what we do.

FUSION could not have happened without the artistic and organisational expertise of artists, arts consultants and Artlink. The Hospital Arts Consortium is grateful to them. Likewise thanks are due to Artlink Director, Jan-Bert van den Berg, Artlink Hospital Arts Co-ordinator Kirsty Lorenz, the Endowment Trustees of the Lothian NHS Trusts who supported the project, and of course to the National Lottery New Directions Fund, administered by the Scottish Arts Council.

Jim Eunson, for The Hospital Arts Consortium

Introduction

In 1998, when the FUSION programme was first devised, Artlink had been working within hospitals for fourteen years. Artlink's work had developed from an arts access and information service in its very early years to an organisation with three distinct areas of interest: a volunteer escort to arts service, arts in the community and art in hospitals. Initially work undertaken in hospitals was based on short-term projects devised and co-ordinated by a part-time worker. In 1995, Artlink gained support from four NHS Trusts and the Scottish Arts Council to establish a full-time Hospital Arts Co-ordinator post. The remit for this job was to develop and programme hospital arts galleries, and to build on the experience of past arts projects and residencies to develop a new programme of art work for the NHS Trusts. As a result of Artlink's growing involvement in project work over the following years, a clear understanding emerged that there was great potential for a longer-term approach to the arts in these hospitals. In 1997, the Lothian Hospital Arts Consortium was formed, with the intention of creating greater cohesion in the arts programme, and of making a bid to the arts lottery. In 1999, funding was approved by the Scottish Arts Council National Lottery New Directions Fund for FUSION, a two-year programme of collaborative art work with patients and departments in the hospitals of Edinburgh and the Lothians.

The development of the FUSION project was also a result of other influences. During the early and mid-1990s policies of care in the community had a significant impact on the nature of healthcare and social provision. The emphasis changed from providing healthcare services in large institutions to community based social provision in small homes dispersed throughout the Lothians. These changes affected the nature of services provided to individuals with disabilities and specific support needs, with a greater emphasis on personalised care planning and support services. Although these developments have been a positive experience for most, some individuals continue to experience exclusion from participation either within existing institutions or their new homes in the community. At the same time, a growing appreciation and understanding of artists pursuing a community-based or socially engaged arts practice emerged within Artlink and contact was made with the Littoral network and other arts agencies pursuing a socially engaged approach.

As a result of these varied influences, Artlink devised programmes which sought to use artists' skills in looking at different ways of responding to these complex issues, using involvement in the arts to create a positive public profile for the individual. For some programmes this meant the artist continued to work as facilitator, and for others it meant investigation of the process itself. Throughout all these programmes the participant is at the centre of the art-making, with their concerns, interests and issues being adopted and merged with the interests of the artists. We have sought to learn from these models, using the participants' experiences to influence the development of new approaches, devising distinct models of practice whose strategies of engagement are integral to the development of a shared 'aesthetic' language. Consequently, methods of arts practice within Artlink have become more diverse and challenging, changing perceptions of the role of art within healthcare and the role of artist as facilitator.

To this end FUSION is in fact a fusion of ways of working within Artlink as a whole – a bringing together of different forms of practice identified within key areas of Artlink's experience. By using collaboration as its main approach, it has shifted emphasis from the traditional production of objects for marketing and consumption to a greater awareness of the social role of art, identifying more closely with the process or relationship formed than with the product itself. The programme has investigated ways in which the artist could submerge their own identity within collaborative practice, finding new ways for the individual patient or hospital department to utilise the artist's expertise. Out of this FUSION has developed two distinct methods of practice: **Collaborations** and **Commissions**. In developing the programme the overall success of FUSION was dependent upon how the artist achieved real and substantive interactions. These can be defined as the ways in which they brought individuals and departments into the process, and how that process could redefine the relationship between artist, non-artist and the work of art. This collaborative approach, intrinsic to FUSION practice, has raised critical questions regarding the role of the artist within these resources and the outcome of the artwork itself.

At points within the programme there has been concern that collaborative practice could lead to unclear relationships, that working in collaboration might lead to the manipulation of vulnerable people and the creation of arts practice that exploited the individuals' interests. Within FUSION **Collaborations** the positive relationship formed between the artist and participant, based on mutual understanding and trust, has been the key to the success of the programme. The artists continually questioned the nature of the collaboration, seeking in response to find new ways in which the patient could utilise the artist's expertise and vice versa. Great emphasis was placed on taking the time to gain an understanding of each individual, on discovering individual interests and on mutually identifying the appropriate methods with which to work. Much of this activity goes unseen, and it can take a year or more of facilitative workshops in order to gain mutual trust – months of artists visiting individuals on wards, working with them until they become confident enough in their own abilities to work in partnership with the artists. The importance and quality of these relationships formed and of the collaborative work undertaken, are reflected in the end products.

Using similar principles of collaboration, the FUSION **Commissions** used the relationships formed between artist, hospital staff and patient as the basis for production of artworks for identified departments within the Royal Infirmary, Western General and St John's at Howden Hospitals. The Commissions programme had a clearly phased approach in developing a relationship with the departments to ensure an 'engaged' process. This approach has resulted in artworks within departments which have relevance, and which were produced as part of a collaborative process. However, working in busy hospital departments within limited timescales necessitated a different approach. In response to limited time, the artist had to shift emphasis from working within hospital departments to using their research from those departments as the basis for the creation of a lasting product of that interaction. In some cases, the artists utilised the skills of hospital staff in the making of the final artwork – for example in plastic surgery at St John's. Other works clearly react to the specific environment and function of the department – the use of aromatherapy oils and scented plants in the Eye Pavilion are integral to the art work.

It is clear that the arts have a valuable and specific role within healthcare. On an individual level the arts highlight the unique skills and qualities of the people creating the work, and can give a voice or draw attention to a specific issue. For patients in these hospitals, it has been very important that these opportunities do not stop, and that their desire to communicate and express themselves does not fit into any specific funding time-frame. In planning for the future, there is also a need to reflect on the whole experience, allowing all those involved in the FUSION project to influence its future direction. What is very clear is that, by allowing time to build up meaningful, collaborative relationships, and by utilising all the unique skills available within those relationships, important work is created – work that merges both community and fine art practice, positioning itself perhaps as a hybrid activity. A lot of work remains to be done if this type of practice is to gain a wider critical appreciation, and for it to be taken out of its marginalised position.

Jan-Bert van den Berg, Director and Alison Stirling, Projects Director
Artlink, Edinburgh

Right: Anne Elliot and Margaret J Cairns

Collaborations

Common sense is a balance between nature and the working of the brain. The balance can be maintained in most people. But when you are a baby you haven't any common sense, you react until you are able to control the faculties of your hands and legs and feet. Your eyes are your guidance and your parents give them all the love that they need until you get common sense. Once you get common sense you grow up a bit and get characteristics of your own.

Common sense is known in everyone, in little doses in some. Some have got wits that are not able to relate very well to things around them, and make common sense difficult. Common sense is seen in people who have handicaps and get into dangerous situations and come out of it because their common sense stops them from being injured. This is called knowledge of the brain and the body.

Knowledge of the brain and the body relate to each other in common sense. The brain relates to the whole body from an early age and casts itself to give a nervous system. The nervous system helps you relate to other people and relate to your surroundings, it helps you guide your body.

Jeanette Bell/Kate Gray
Common Sense from the
series *Knowledge,* 2001

Series of seven canvas dolls made as copies of drawings by Jeanette. Each doll is accompanied by a recorded monologue written by Jeanette and read by various hospital workers.

But common sense is needed when it comes to going into kitchens and into roadways and learning to drive...because common sense can lead to knowledge. Knowledge can be a little harmful if its practised from memory and not from truth. Memory of what you thought you saw and memory of what you think you should do, instead of memory of what is realistic and of what is the correct way.

Extract from *Common Sense* by Jeanette Bell

Jeanette Bell / Kate Gray
Cover, 2001

Forty-six felt badges sewn onto a second hand
blanket. The images embroidered on
the badges are exact copies of drawings
by Jeanette.

Kate Stewart / Kate Gray
Ikebana, 2000

Series of three large format photographs of ikebana flower arrangements
commissioned for wards 1, 3 and 5 of the Royal Edinburgh Hospital.

AS/Kate Gray
322 x 285, 2002

250 cast plaster bricks made as replicas of
hospitals and homes in which AS has lived.
The bricks are used to construct a room-shaped
space to the exact dimensions of AS's current
room.

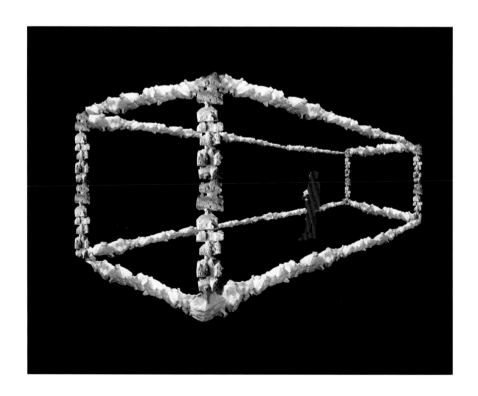

SUNSTROKE

M J CAIRNS

Two women, born in the 1920's, related but of totally different backgrounds start out in life knowing nothing about the other. Gradually the elder of the two is disastrously attracted to the opposite sex and makes some surprising discoveries, which awakens her own obsessive desire to destroy the unenlightened younger one. Set in the West Country at the end of the first world war how much is an individuals make-up due to nature or nurture?

Previous page:
Margaret J Cairns / Anne Elliot and Kate Gray
Mobile Library, 2001

Temporary reference library housed in a trailer with a Vespa scooter, customised with transferred drawings by Margaret.

Above and opposite:
Margaret J Cairns / Anne Elliot and Kate Gray
57 Titles, 57 Texts, 57 Drawings, 2001

Bound collections of book covers designed by Margaret. The covers feature pictures of iconic women accompanied by text extracted from romantic novels. The books are retitled by Margaret, and will be circulated by West Lothian Libraries.

ENGLISHM

t World

KENNETH GRIFFITH

RICHARD E. GRAN

57 TITLES

DARIES GUPPY — ROLL THE DICE

DOUGLAS HAIG 1861-1928 — De Groot

ETER HALL — MAKING AN EXHIBITION OF MY

WII

ALISTAI

Gloria

RICHARD — Lord of th

Clive J

MARTIN JA

Why My F

Jocky / Anne Elliot
Above: *As Art is to be Criticised,
Colorado Freeway, 2000*
Opposite: *As Art is to be Criticised,
View from New York*, 2001

Two installations, each comprising a painting by
Jocky accompanied by two video monitors. One
monitor shows Jocky explaining his work while
the other documents a discussion of the work by
a panel of critics.

Andrew Gemmell / Anne Elliot
Above: *Colouring–In Book*, 1999 ongoing
Opposite: *Sketchbook*, 1999 ongoing

Series of colouring–in books and sketchbooks
featuring drawings by Andrew in felt pen.

Jim Duncan / Anne Elliot
6pm : bartering, 2001

A series of six meals prepared for invited guests.
The meals were bought, cooked, eaten and
documented by Jim Duncan and Anne Elliot.

MY FATHER
IS THE WISEMAN
OF THE VILLAGE

Nicky Barrett / Kate Gray
My father is the wise man of the village, 2001

Neon work created from one of a series of drawings by Nicky Barrett.

Patrick Hoey / Paul Barham
Viscount, 2001

Temporary site drawing in the grounds of
Bangour Village Hospital. A second site
drawing has been commissioned as part of
My father is the wise man of the village at
The Fruitmarket Gallery.

Below and opposite: Evelyn Whitefield / Anne Elliot and Michelle Naismith
The thing to remember in this is balance, 2001
Telecined 16mm film

Free style

Francis McKee

The FUSION programme lies within a long and complex history of artistic collaborations in medical settings. The earliest collaborations have their roots in the anatomical mapping of the body – a project that for centuries involved surgeons and artists creating images that were both scientifically meaningful and culturally resonant. In this history scientists have often been seduced by the art of representation and artists, in their turn, have become fascinated by the technology and insights of medicine.

For at least as long, there has been another history of medicine and art. In the depiction of melancholy and depression, the artist is also the one who experiences the illness or collaborates closely with others who have encountered it. While the anatomical illustrators more often succeeded in producing work that was useful for science, this second history produced something more intangible – works of art that could range from Burton's *Anatomy of Melancholy* to Shakespeare's *Hamlet*, or Lawrence Sterne's *Tristram Shandy*, Goya's *Caprichio's*, Munch's *The Scream* or the rich history of the blues.

As technology advanced, however, medicine and art gradually parted ways. Anatomists now find it more useful to distribute computer enhanced photographs of the body on the internet, or to employ magnetic resonance imaging to explore the functions of the brain. Drawing, painting and eventually even photography were seen as too imprecise for the needs of contemporary science. For artists, opportunities to work in the world of science or medicine became increasingly rare.

Equally, as the twentieth-century avant-garde passed from cubism to surrealism, from abstract expressionism to minimalism, there seemed little that art could usefully contribute to any collaboration beyond its own world. Not only that, but the idea of collaboration itself became suspect. Unlike the renaissance 'masters', who employed teams of workers in their various schools to contribute to the overall effect of a painting, the modern artist was seen as a lone individual. Each work was perceived to be an intimate expression of a unique personality. In this new context the notion of collaboration simply created confusion and anxiety. In a collaborative art work it was difficult – if not impossible – to distinguish the work of each of the artists. Each artist's unique form of expression was seen to be diluted by its combination with the work of another – an elimination of potential rather than a positive creation. Even in the career of Andy Warhol (an artist who returned to the factory concept of production), his attempts to collaborate on joint paintings with Jean-Michel Basquiat were met with confusion and hostility. As collaborations the paintings could not be sold for as much as a solo work by either artist, and they were persistently dismissed as publicity gimmicks rather than art.

Oddly, the unstoppable rise of the artist as 'lone genius' was paralleled by the appearance of the 'outsider' artist. 'Art brut', or outsider art, was a genre pioneered by Jean Dubuffet, a French artist inspired by the work being produced in psychiatric hospitals in Switzerland in the late 1940s. Outsider artists were seen as beyond the constraints of the academy and the rules of contemporary art practice. Drawing on the melancholic tradition, this new conception of the artist mirrored the development of the unique loner in the mainstream art world, and in some ways provided a foundation for that development. The outsider artist was seen to be equally individualistic, to the point that the art work was obsessive, flowing compulsively from the artist's deepest instincts – almost beyond rational control. The image of such artists was neatly summed up in a description of one of the first stars of this genre, Adolf Wölfli, who claimed, "He was completely free to express himself, entirely uninhibited by rules. That results in a nearly wild mode of expression"[1].

Dubuffet and Wölfli were to establish a pattern that continued to repeat itself throughout the second half of the twentieth century. When the sculptor Jean Tinguely discovered the primitively made machines of Heinrich Anton Müller in the courtyard of a psychiatric hospital, he declared "They impressed him as much as Müller's story... It was no longer a question of art as merchandise or art as a material object, but art as a pure form of expression, an art that was free of social rank"[2]. What's interesting in Tinguely's assessment is his fascination with Müller's illness, which is as important as the art work itself, confirming its unique and exotic roots. The objects too are seen as 'a pure form of expression' free of social and artistic constraints.

Such a position couldn't be held for long. It was clear, even from their subject matter, that these 'pure' artists were just as much influenced by the society around them as anyone else. Once they gained critical attention and fame, as Wölfli did, it became even more obvious that they then began to think of themselves as 'artists' and the issue quickly evolved into one of where to place them in relation to the mainstream.

For curators such as Harald Szeemann and Pontus Hulten the answer was to incorporate art brut into exhibitions with other contemporary artists, highlighting similarities in their formal approach or in their process of making. For Szeemann, this was a way of, "giving value to individual expression and dispensing with the presentation of a case"[3]. In this new context, the artist as individual maker was still confirmed, but at least now it was admitted that cultural influence and artistic thought did not stop at the entrance to a hospital.

Despite Szeemann's useful separation of art from case history, many questions still remain around the placement of art and artists in hospitals today. Is art therapeutic, for example, or is the process of making art therapeutic? Should the completed object be the focus of such work, and should it be judged by the same criteria as any other contemporary art? And, vitally, what is the status of collaboration in such

circumstances? Do we try to separate the artist from their collaborator or do we see the relationship as an equal creative partnership? Is the collaborative process primarily therapeutic or can it be a real creative enterprise?

Just as importantly, such collaborations force viewers of the work to consider their own expectations and viewing habits. In museums and galleries we constantly see objects abstracted from their original context, purpose and environment. Not only that, but many of the images we consider art – such as Giotto's murals – are known to most of us only as reproductions, divorced from their proper viewing conditions. In these circumstances the object becomes the focus of attention, and, in a reductive process, art is reduced to being a finished product. What is lost is a sense of the communal process that a work of art is engaged in. Giotto's murals in the Arena chapel in Padua were never conceived of 'just as art', but as art that decorated the walls of a space where religious rites were conducted and spirituality was expressed. Likewise a Vermeer, a Stubbs or a Cézanne was a work that was designed to be incorporated into different styles of domestic life. All of these works acknowledged the world beyond art, and the creation of the object was just one stage in an artistic process that went on to include the work in its eventual location.

With the gradual rise of the white cube gallery, this context and sense of communal process was lost. Without it, the artwork as commodity gained increasing importance and the production of objects was seen as a 'career'. Since the 1970s there have been a succession of artists who have rebelled against these constraints. Robert Smithson, in his essay 'Cultural Confinement' (1972), famously argued against the 'fraudulent categories' imposed on contemporary artists and the clinical qualities of the white cube, stating that:

A work of art when placed in a gallery loses its charge, and becomes a portable object or surface disengaged from the outside world. A vacant white room with lights is still a submission to the neutral. Works of art seen in such spaces seem to be going through a kind of aesthetic convalescence. They are looked upon as so many inanimate invalids, waiting for critics to pronounce them curable or incurable.[4]

It is ironic, then, that today it is the hospital itself that offers an escape from this cultural confinement. Hospitals thrive on continuous process, on communal values and a system designed around essential human situations of health, life and death. For an artist entering such an environment, the usefulness of their occupation is immediately questioned and art is forced to confront a raw world. To collaborate in such situations becomes even more compelling, and often for reasons that are seldom mentioned. Anyone who has been seriously ill knows the invisibility that descends on the sick – to be ill in our society is to be irrelevant. If any gain can be taken from this, it is probably the space that it allows for breaking the rules – to make art in such a situation is not a career strategy, and therefore the pressure of the marketplace and the critics are lessened.

The Mozart Effect

The possible health benefits of the music of Mozart were assessed in the April 2001 edition of the Journal of the Royal Society of Medicine. There has been controversy about the benefits ever since researchers claimed that listening to the *K.448* piano sonata improved spatial reasoning skills. Later research suggested that *K.448* can reduce the number of seizures in people with epilepsy. Professor John Jenkins assesses international evidence on the effect of music on the brain, and calls for more work to be done to discover the key ingredient in the 'Mozart Effect'.

The original Mozart Effect study in 1993 assessed volunteers' spatial reasoning after listening to sonata *K.448*, relaxation tapes or silence. Results suggested that just ten minutes of Mozart's music improved their performance on tasks such as paper-

cutting and folding. Later studies found that rats negotiated a maze faster after hearing *K.448* than rats who were played white noise, silence, or minimalist music. Elsewhere, children taught a keyboard instrument for six months, learning simple melodies (including Mozart), did better on spatial-temporal tests than children who spent the same time working with computers.

In a collaborative video work by Dougie Lawrence, Robert Bridges and Michelle Naismith, we see two images: one of a young man stripped to the waist, conducting an invisible orchestra in a formal garden; the other of a woman seen only from the back in a freeze-frame pose in front of a small orchard. Her arms are raised as if to conduct, and at a certain point the video releases her into movement, while the alternative image of the young man freezes in mid-motion. Mozart's *K.448* continues to play throughout as the screens alternate between movement and stasis.

Certainly the work alludes to the newly discovered improving effects of Mozart's music on spatial reasoning, but it quickly goes beyond this to reflect on the making of the videos themselves and the dynamics of collaboration. It is possible to interpret the videos as an expression of the common belief that in a collaboration one ego will dominate the other as one figure freezes and another acts. The work is much richer than that however and it is equally possible to see one collaborator supporting the other, taking up the task when the other stumbles. More than that, the video pushes beyond the tidy boundaries of the medical research on Mozart. Robert, stripped to the waist outdoors, recalls the techno scene more than the classical concert hall – an image that highlights the researchers' decision to use classical music in the experiment. Somehow the discovery that Mozart and Bach are good for us is predictable and carries the implicit suggestion that music such as techno probably won't help our spatial awareness. All of which brings us back to the issue of art as therapy and the danger that art which disorientates us may be considered less important.

Opposite and right:
Dougie Lawrence / Robert Bridges and Michelle Naismith
K.448, 2001
Two synchronised digital video projections accompanied
by sound

Just as *K.448* neatly frames these questions, so many of the other FUSION projects address issues of structure, order and the questioning of art and its role in the world. This can be seen most clearly perhaps in the collaboration between Jocky and Anne Elliot, *As Art is to be Criticised*. There Jocky's paintings are accompanied by two videos – one in which he explains the work and another in which a panel of critics discusses it. These videos shift the emphasis of the piece away from the notion of a finished object to a more fluid concept of art in constant process, changing with time, the viewer's subjectivity, and the environment in which it is shown. In this context, the painting as object is simply one stage in a longer process that includes the critique and continuous redefinition of art.

Kate Stewart's collaboration with Kate Gray approaches the issue of criticism and environment from the opposite direction. Here, the art work acts as critic through a series of ikebana installations in various recreational areas of a hospital. Ikebana – the japanese art of flower arranging – draws on and critiques the space in which it is shown. One history of the form describes it as follows:

The various ikebana styles include countless methods of selecting flowers and vases. But they all involve a flexible decision-making process that emphasizes harmony with the situation, such as the purpose of the ikebana arrangement, the nature of the space where it will be displayed, the season and the weather. In ikebana, vases serve as the earth for the plant materials, and they are vitally important factors that help to determine the beauty of the ikebana arrangement.[5]

It is this critical decision-making process that is the key element of *Ikebana*. Kate Stewart and Kate Gray assessed the environment in which the work was displayed, and produced installations which highlight the shoddy and impoverished nature of contemporary institutional architecture and decor. Their ikebana combines beauty with rebuke.

What links so many of the collaborations in FUSION is this sense of critical framing which demands that we consider the context as well as the work. Kate Gray's projects with both Jeanette Bell and AS also demonstrate this point. In one monologue accompanying the dolls in *Knowledge* the voice states that, "Knowledge of the brain and the body relate to each other in common sense... the nervous system helps you relate to other people and relate to your surroundings". Jeanette's other piece, *Cover*, reproduces forty-six of her drawings on felt badges which are then sewn onto a second-hand blanket, transposing the original work and reframing it on a blanket, and subsequently on a photograph of the blanket in a landscape. Knowledge here is being filtered and framed, removing it from the easy classification of art brut, and blurring the distinction of each of the collaborator's contributions. Likewise, in *322 x 285,* the bricks shaped as hospitals are used to reconstruct the dimensions of AS's current room in a knowing, fractal autobiography.

Perhaps the two most explicit collaborations in terms of self-awareness and spatial expression are those involving Anne Elliot and Michelle Naismith; firstly with Sandra Kinsey and secondly with Evelyn White. In Elliot and Naismith's project with Kinsey – *Sandra, portrait of a bargain hunter* – we find ourselves watching a video in which the three collaborators discuss a schedule for the making of the film we are now viewing. To complicate matters further, they are themselves looking at some footage of Sandra Kinsey, which will appear later in the same film. At this point time seems to be folding in on itself, but the most striking moments of the video are the various shots of Sandra singing old standards such as 'Bye Bye Blackbird'. Here, the work captures the other-worldly rhythm of residency in a hospital where illness removes you from the urgency and pressure of contemporary life. The beauty and simplicity of these moments echo Elliot and Naismith's other collaboration with Evelyn Whitefield – *The thing to remember in this is balance.* Again, the focus on order is important in their video of two tango dancers dancing in a caravan at sunset within the hospital grounds. The lyricism of the piece, the serenity of the scene and the use

of 16mm film to provide depth and luminosity all combine to imply a sense of mental space and harmony – a personal order that can be found within the larger context of the hospital.

Interestingly, this desire to construct a more peaceful inner space runs through almost all of the artists commissions in the FUSION project. It is perhaps most apparent in Dalziel + Scullion's specially designed *Sanctuary Furniture* which has its origins in their recognition of the emotional dislocation experienced by many hospital visitors:

By the end of our visit we had become aware that for many of the people who will enter the Chaplaincy / Sanctuary space, their ordinary day to day lives may have somehow been put on hold – a suspended animation if you like – whilst the immediacy of the challenges they face take precedence.

For many of the artists placed within hospital departments, the engagement with FUSION meant that their own daily working habits were placed in a kind of suspended animation as process began to take precedence over production. Speaking of her project at the Royal Infirmary, Michèle Lazenby stated:

Realising that the process of engagement could have a greater impact on some people or be more meaningful than the final artwork has made me re-evaluate ... and resolve to take a Zen approach (i.e. endeavour to stay focused on the present and open to what is happening...)

Similarly, for Zoe Walker and Anne Morrison, the busyness of dedicated and caring health workers forced a reassessment of art's role in such an environment. The importance of the work they were seeing – in terms of life, death and pain – demanded a more urgent response to their environment than any gallery or artworld situation. For some of the other artists, this situation generated a utilitarian approach – Rachel Mimiec thought, "it feels very much like starting a new job..." while Catriona Grant pointed out that, "the staff accepted me as a worker with a valuable role to play within the department".

What is immediately clear from all of the Commissions is the willingness of the artists and medical staff to work together, and their belief in the potential benefits of the Commissions. Effectively what we are seeing in such situations is a renegotiation of the centuries-old collaboration between doctor and artist. Now, however, the situation is more diffuse. Rather than one doctor or anatomist working in relative isolation, the artist encounters teams, departmental networks and a technological infrastructure.

Stephen Skrynka's *Bladder Music* offers one example of how the FUSION artists formulated a creative response in this environment. Skrynka begins by gathering the patients' urine flow charts which are then converted to musical compositions, combining the patients' favourite tunes with the flow graphs. The result – a series of 'signature' tunes for each patient – is played through a 'family' of small sculptures reminiscent of urine flasks and other paraphernalia of Urology. The sculptures were sited throughout the department, broadcasting this new, hybrid music.

In making this, Skrynka evolved a working process that seems to shadow that of the departmental staff. He starts from the same database of information – the patients' flow charts – and then interprets and transforms the information with the help of Alistair MacDonald, working on the electro-acoustics and composition, and Bob Farrell on computer programming and chart mapping. The data undergoes a metamorphosis – a lateral move that would not normally be possible in scientific procedure – to create music for staff and patients alike. The notion of a 'signature' tune, in particular, gains importance, reaffirming the patient's identity in a hospital context – which is an environment that, even unwittingly, can undermine the patient's sense of worth. There is also a lightness of touch to the project that helps to carry it off as Skrynka converts urine into music – an alchemical sleight of hand that would arouse envy amongst medieval doctors.

Bladder Music is typical of the FUSION Commissions in the inventiveness of its response to an unusual context. This is one of the great strengths of the project. What all the FUSION works share is a displacement from the standard preconceptions of today's artworld, and a self-awareness that also manages to elude the usual categorisations of the 'outsider', or art as therapy. The different rythyms of hospital life have had a clear influence on all of the artists, opening up a new creative space for them. This has been reinforced by the networks of people and the continuous medical process they have encountered. What is perhaps just as striking, though, is the enthusiasm of the medical staff for these projects – indicating changes in medicine that now seem to offer new collaborative opportunities for artists. Perhaps the role of technology has changed in some significant way to permit this, or perhaps the scientists' awareness of the limits of technology have become more acute. Thus, while it is possible to see a critical edge to almost all of the FUSION projects that challenges the narrow confines of the contemporary art experience, they can also help chart the evolving relationship between art, doctor and scientist.

Francis McKee is a writer and curator based in Glasgow

1   Per Norgard recorded by Jean-Pierre Amann in *Concert du monde*, Radio Suisse Romande, 2 February 1993
2   Pontus Hulten, Jean Tinguely, *Meta* (Paris, 1773) p. 171
3   Harald Szeemann, *Ein neues Museum im Lausanne. Die 'Collection de l'Art Brut', Indivuelle Mythologien* (Berlin, 1985), p.46.
4   *Robert Smithson: The Collected Writings*, Ed. Jack Flam,(University of California Press, 1996) p.154-55
5   Daniela Jost, *Ikebana Training and Accessories* website (www.geocities.com/roman.jost/Ikebana_History_English.htm)

Commissions

Stephen Skrynka
Bladder Music, 2001
Painted acrylic resin, speakers, CD player
Nurse Led Urology
Western General Hospital, Edinburgh

In *Bladder Music* patients' urine flow charts are converted into musical compositions. By combining their favourite tune with their flow graph, a 'signature tune' is created for each patient. The compositions are played through a 'family' of small sculptures located throughout the Urology Department on trolleys in waiting rooms, wards and corridors.

Rachel Mimiec
Paper Hearts, 2001
Digital prints and artists' books
Cardiology Department
Royal Infirmary of Edinburgh

Origami hearts made over a period of three days
by the artist and given to approximately eighty
patients and staff in the department.
A selection of these were photographed and
paired with the artist's collage works, and
displayed on the walls of the day room of ward
31 and the reception corridor in Cardiology.

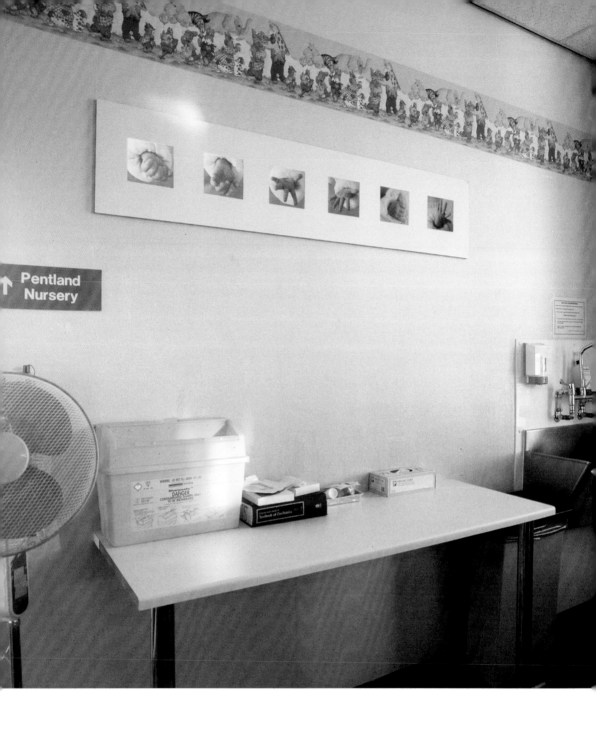

Janie Nicoll
Leylah, 2001
Lambda digital prints on MDF
Neo Natal Unit
Simpson Memorial Maternity Pavillion
Royal Infirmary of Edinburgh

Leylah is a photographic tableau of the hands
of premature babies, derived from stills of video
footage taken in the Neo Natal Unit. The work is
a prototype for a series of five works that will be
installed in the new Royal Infirmary at Little
France, Edinburgh.

Anne Morrison
Above: *Grasslands (wish)*, 2001
Opposite: *Light Traces,* 2001
Both oil on canvas
Liver Transplant Unit / Haematology
Royal Infirmary of Edinburgh

Series of small oil paintings placed in the Haematology and Liver
Transplant Units. The paintings' organic forms represent a world
in microcosm/macrocosm. Five series were produced in total.

Dalziel + Scullion
Sanctuary Furniture, 2001
Beech table and lamps
Chaplaincy Department
Royal Infirmary of Edinburgh

The work comprises a beech wood table with
coloured glass insert under which rhythmic
patterns of light are visible. The work is
accompanied by two free standing lamps, each
with printed photographic drop paper shades.

Catriona Grant
Oneironauts 2001
Lambda prints
The Sleep Centre
Royal Infirmary of Edinburgh

Series of paired photographic prints, featuring
images captured from closed circuit television
footage of patients in the sleep centre, and
specially created dream sequences shot in the
wards of the Royal Infirmary. The work is sited in
the day room of the Sleep Centre.

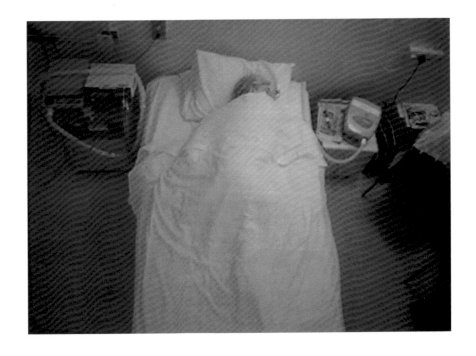

Zoe Walker in collaboration with Gill Thompson
Honeysuckle for St John's, 2001
Lightboxes with transparencies, display case
with silicon, wire and flock honeysuckle
Plastic Surgery
St John's Hospital, Livingston

Artificial honeysuckle buds made by Maxillofacial technician Gill Thompson
were repositioned on the original bush and photographed by Zoe Walker.
This image is presented as a light-box, with a second lightbox showing
documentation of the process of making the honeysuckle bud. A display
case contains a new completely fake honeysuckle flower.

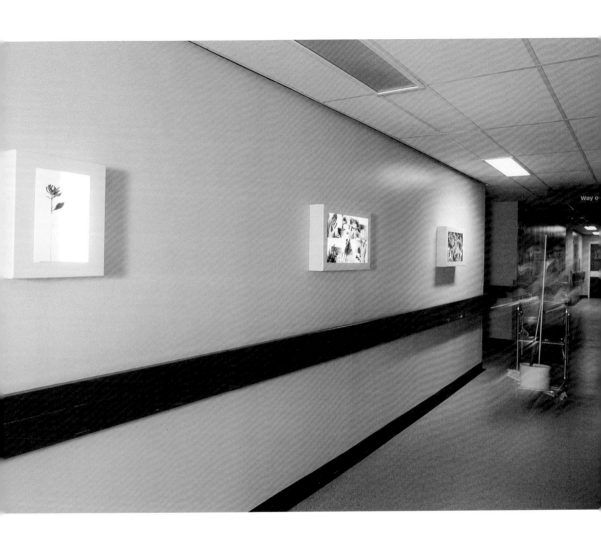

Michèle Lazenby
Untitled, 2001
Lightboxes, essential oils and jasmine
Eye Pavillion
Royal Infirmary of Edinburgh

Wooden planter containing jasmine plants placed at the
entrance to the Eye Pavilion. This was accompanied by
two circular light boxes mounted on walls painted in
complimentary colours, and essential oils in burners
located at the two reception desks on the ground floor.
The colours and aromas were selected to assist visitors
(particularly the visually impaired) with orientation, and to
promote a more soothing and uplifting environment for
staff and patients.

List of Works: Collaborations

Page 10
Jeanette Bell / Kate Gray
Knowledge (Common Sense), 2001
Seven dolls with monologues
50 x 25cm each

Also in series:
Money, Money, Money
Religious Knowledge
First Aid
Black Magic
Green Cross Code
Safety First
Photo: Alan Dimmick

Pages 12–13
Jeanette Bell / Kate Gray
Cover, 2000
Blanket with embroidered patches
C type print
180 x 180cm
Photo: Anne Elliot

Pages 14–15
Kate Stewart / Kate Gray
Ikebana, 2000
C type prints
90 x 90cm each
Photo: Kate Gray

Pages 16–17
AS / Kate Gray
322 x 285, 2002
250 cast plaster bricks
322 x 285 x 264cm
Photo: Alan Dimmick
Computer model: Kate Gray

Pages 18–19
Margaret J Cairns / Anne Elliot
and Kate Gray
Mobile Library, 2001
Customised scooter, trailer and helmet
137 x 79 x 490cm
Photo: Anne Elliot

Pages 20–21
Margaret J Cairns / Anne Elliot
and Kate Gray
57 Titles, 57 Texts, 57 Drawings, 2001
Inkjet prints
Edition of four A4 books
Photo: Alan Dimmick, Anne Elliot

Pages 22–23
Jocky / Anne Elliot
As Art is to be Criticised,
Colorado Freeway, 2000 (p.24)
Acrylic on MDF, two video monitors
160 x 140cm
Photo: Anne Elliot

As Art is to be Criticised,
View from New York, 2001 (p.25)
Acrylic on MDF, two video monitors
160 x 140cm
Photo: Alan Dimmick

Pages 24–25
Andrew Gemmell
Colouring-In Book,
ongoing project (p.26)
Felt pen on printed paper
30 x 18cm
Photo: Alan Dimmick

Sketchbook, ongoing project (p.27)
Felt pen on printed paper
30 x 18cm
Photo: Alan Dimmick

Pages 26–27
Jim Duncan / Anne Elliot
6pm : bartering, 2001
Lightbox with digital colour duratrans
203 x 114cm
Photo: Anne Elliot

Page 28–29
Nicky Barrett / Kate Gray
My father is the wise man
of the village, 2001

Neon wall text
239 x 225cm
Photo: Alan Dimmick

Pages 30-31
Patrick Hoey / Paul Barham
Viscount, 2001
Site drawing, gaffa tape
30 x 10m
Photo: Anne Elliot

Pages 32-33
Evelyn Whitefield / Anne Elliot
and Michelle Naismith
The thing to remember in this
is balance, 2001
Telecined 16mm colour film
projection with sound, 3.5 minutes
Film still: Louise Crawford

Page 36
Lorraine Boyd / Anne Elliot
and Michelle Naismith
Three single ladies, 2001
Digital colour video with sound
20 minutes

Pages 38–39
Dougie Lawrence / Robert Bridges
and Michelle Naismith
K.448, 2001
Two synchronised colour digital
video projections with sound
6 minutes

Page 41
Sandra Kinsey / Anne Elliot
and Michelle Naismith
Sandra, portrait of a bargain hunter
2000–01
Digital video with sound
7.5 minutes

List of Works: Commissions

Pages 44–45
Stephen Skrynka
Bladder Music, 2001
Painted acrylic resin, speakers,
CD player
15 x 20cm each (approx.)

Urology Department
Western General, Edinburgh
Key person: Mr Laurence Stewart
The sound aspect of this project was
developed in collaboration with Dr Alistair
MacDonald Head of Electro Acoustic
Composition, RSAMD, Glasgow.
Computer programming and mapping of
flow charts by Bob Farrell
The artist would like to thank:
Sister Mary Smith, Sister Chris Harris,
Dr Sami Moussa and David Wright
Photo: Alan Dimmick

Pages 46–47
Rachel Mimiec
Paper Hearts, 2001
Digital prints and artist books
51 x 23cms each print

Cardiology Department
Royal Infirmary of Edinburgh
Key people: Kenny Branny,
Lynn McDonald
The artist would like to thank: Pat Wynne
Photo: Alan Dimmick, Rachel Mimiec

Pages 48–49
Janie Nicoll
Leylah, 2001

Also in series:
Joseph, 2001, *Alexander*, 2001,
Kieran, 2001, *Sarah*, 2001
Lambda Digital prints on MDF
Five panels, 160cm x 35cm

Neo Natal Unit
Simpson Memorial Maternity Pavillion
Royal Infirmary of Edinburgh
Key person: Dr Iain Laing
Photo: Alan Dimmick, Janie Nicoll

Pages 50–51
Anne Morrison
Grasslands (wish), 2001 (p.50)
Oil on canvas
Series of five, 27 x 27cm each

Light Traces, 2001 (p.51)
Oil on canvas
Series of four, 27 x 25cm each

Also in series:
Location (land and sky), 2001
Oil on canvas
Series of four, 27 x 25cm each
Grasslands, 2001
Oil on canvas
Series of two, 27 x 25cm each
Grasslands, 2001
Oil on canvas
Series of two, 27 x 25cm each

Haematology / Liver Transplant Unit
Royal Infirmary of Edinburgh
Key people: Catriona Crow
(Haematology), Sister Caroline
Stephenson (Transplant Unit)
The artist would like to thank:
Professor Hayes and Ken Simpson
Photo: Alan Dimmick

Pages 52–53
Dalziel + Scullion
Sanctuary Furniture, 2001
Beech table and lamps
Table 56 x 80 x 60cm
Two lamps each 173 x 21cm

Chaplaincy
Royal Infirmary of Edinburgh
Key people: Ewan Kelly, Ian Telford,
Anne Mulligan
Photo: Alan Dimmick

Pages 54–55
Catriona Grant
Oneironauts, 2001
Lambda prints
13 x 18cm

Sleep Centre
Royal Infirmary of Edinburgh
Key person: Heather Engleman
The artist would like to thank:
Marjorie Vennelle, Renata Riha,
Alec Rosie
Photo: Alan Dimmick, Catriona Grant

Pages 56–57
Zoe Walker / Gill Thompson
Honeysuckle for St John's, 2001
Lightboxes with transparencies,
display case with silicon, wire and
flock honeysuckle
65 x 40 x 10cm and 34 x 40 x 10cm

Maxillofacial Unit
Department of Plastic and
Reconstructive Surgery
St John's Hospital, Livingston
Key people: Gill Thompson,
Jeff Millar, Hazel Herd
The artist would like to thank:
Faye McKay, Dr J D Watson,
Jim Eunson, Sister Julia Little
Colin Gray
Photo: Alan Dimmick, Zoe Walker

Pages 58–59
Michèle Lazenby
Untitled, 2001
2 x duratrans on circular lightboxes,
vinyl emulsion paint on walls, bamboo
laminate planter with jasmine, petitgrain
and bergamot essential oils and burner
100cm diameter each

Eye Pavillion
Royal Infirmary of Edinburgh
Key person: Stuart Gairns
The artist would like to thank:
Susan Parker, Sister Margaret
MacDonald and Tim Monroe
Photo: Alan Dimmick

The artists would like to thank all staff
and patients of the various departments
involved in the Commissions programme.

Acknowledgements

FUSION Collaboration Artists
Anne Elliot, team leader
Kate Gray
Michelle Naismith

FUSION Commissions Artists
Dalziel + Scullion
Catriona Grant
Michèle Lazenby
Rachel Mimiec
Anne Morrison
Janie Nicoll
Stephen Skrynka
Zoe Walker

Artlink
Jan-Bert van den Berg, Director
Vanessa Cameron, Administration
Kirsty Lorenz, Hospital Arts
Co-ordinator until May 2001
Alison Stirling, Projects Director

Freelance Specialists
Trevor Cromie, exhibition and
publication / DVD concept and
implementation
Stephen Hurrel, FUSION
Commissions Co-ordinator
Lucy Shorrocks, FUSION Press
and Publicity

Lothian Hospital Arts Consortium
Tom Arnott, Lothian Primary Care
NHS Trust
Louise Birrel, Lothian Primary Care
NHS Trust
Jim Eunson, West Lothian Healthcare
NHS Trust
Iain Laing, Lothian University Hospitals
NHS Trust

Sponsors
55degrees for production and playback
support as part of 55degrees social
responsibility remit
Ernie Lomont, Calton Contracts

(sponsorship in kind, collaborations)
Mark Brown, Photobition B & S
(sponsorship in kind, collaborations)

Collaborators
Leslie Ahmed
Nicky Barrett
Jeanette Bell
Lorraine Boyd
Robert Bridges
Margaret J Cairns
Jim Duncan
Andrew Gemmell
Patrick Hoey
Sandra Kinsey
Dougie Lawrence
Jocky
Kate Stewart
AS
Evelyn Whitefield

Lewis Aarestaad
Ewan Agnew
James Alexander
Carmen Anderson
Wasyl Baran
Karen Bashow
David Brown
Irene Brown
Andrew Cullen
Bruce Delvin
Harry Duffie
Arthur Duncan
Elizabeth Egleton
Tom Findlay
Colin Fortune
Peter Gorman
Anna Gwozdz
Fred Harris
Zena Hudson
Flo Kilpatrick
Janet Kinghorn
James Lamb
Lynda Lamont
Paul Lyon
William Murphy

George Prenty
Ted McCann
Andrew McDonald
Margaret McDougall
Kim McLaughlan
Gwen Mennie
Nan Patterson
David Purves
Joe Shanley
Puran Singh
Anne Speirs
Nessie Whylock
Willie Wilson

**Participating Departments
Collaborations**

Edinburgh
Royal Edinburgh Hospital:
Robert Ferguson Unit
Young Persons Unit
Care of the Elderly, Canaan, Ward 16
Intensive Psychiatric Care Unit
Rehabilitation Wards: Swanston,
Pentland, Northwing, Ettrick, Midmar
Admission Wards 3–6
Professorial Units 1–2
Alcohol Problems Clinic

West Lothian
Bangour Village Hospital, West Lothian:
Bangour Day Centre
Rehabilitation Villas 18, 19, 20, 2 & 5
Intensive Psychiatric Care
Recreational and Social Therapies

St John's Hospital, Livingston:
The Bangour Unit
The Burns Unit
St John's Court Residencies

Tippethill House
Whitburn House
Young Persons Unit, Willowgrove House

Midlothian
Rosslynlee Hospital, Midlothian:
Midlothian Day Hospital

East Lothian
Edenhall Hospital, East Lothian:
Paediatric Occupational Therapy
Care of the Elderly
Eden Day Unit
Crichton Ward

Participating Departments
Commissions
Royal Infirmary of Edinburgh:
Cardiology Department
Chaplaincy Department
Princess Alexandra Eye Pavillion
Haematology
Liver Transplant Unit
Neo Natal Unit, Simpson Memorial
Maternity Pavillion
Sleep Centre

Western General Hospital, Edinburgh:
Urology Department

St. John's Hospital, Livingston:
Department of Plastic and
Reconstructive Surgery

Collaborations Additional Artists
Paul Barham
Keith Farquhar
Valerie Gillies, writer
Diana Hendry, writer
Karen Loughridge
Christina McBride
Calum Stirling

Art Specialists and Consultants
Jason E. Bowman
Maria Brewster
Jenny Brownrigg
Louise Crawford
Dr.Honda
Steve Duval

Karen Guthrie
Deborah Hawthorn
Elizabeth Hobbs
Chad McCail
Billy McCall
Lindsay Perth
Nina Pope
Euan Robertson
Paul Rous & Clea Wallis
Kim Sweet
Caroline Woodley

Volunteers
Emma Barrows
Robbie Chapman
Michaela Dunne
Jonathon Owen
Keith Thompson
Andrew Tullis

Hospital staff
John Banks
Murray Chalmers
Dr Chiswick
Church Centre Staff
Jan Corbett
Mandy Galvin
Dr Shelia Gillfillen
Kathleen Grant
Dr James Hendry
Betty Keith
Sue Robertson
George Strachan

Artlink would like to thank
55degrees, especially
Joseph Briffa, Paul Cameron,
Sam Christopherson, Jamie Cloughley,
Russell Henderson and
Mark Magante

Finally we would like to thank
all the staff and installation team at
The Fruitmarket Gallery, especially
George Gilliland, Juliet Knight,
Elizabeth McLean and Graeme Murray

Catalogue published to accompany *My father is the wise man of the village* an exhibition at The Fruitmarket Gallery, Edinburgh, from 9 February to 30 March 2002. Exhibition curated by Trevor Cromie.

Supported by the Binks Trust, Gordon Fraser Charitable Trust and The Russell Trust.

Catalogue designed and typeset by Elizabeth McLean and Trevor Cromie.

Co-published by:
The Fruitmarket Gallery
45 Market Street
Edinburgh EH1 1DF
Tel: 0131 225 2383
Fax: 0131 220 3130
www.fruitmarket.co.uk

and

Artlink
13a Spittal Street
Edinburgh EH3 9DY
Tel: 0131 229 3555
Fax: 0131 228 5257
www.artlinkedinburgh.co.uk

The Fruitmarket Gallery is subsidised by the Scottish Arts Council.
Scottish Charity No. SC 005576.

Artlink's core programme is subsidised by the City of Edinburgh Council, Midlothian Council, West Lothian Council and the Scottish Arts Council
Scottish Charity No. SCO 06845.

DVD content created and produced by 55degrees and Trevor Cromie

55degrees ltd: creative content consultancy
73 Robertson St
Glasgow G2 8QD
Tel: 0141 222 2855
Fax: 0141 222 2755
www.55degrees.co.uk

To operate web links a software update may be necessary. Contact 55degrees for assistance if required.

Catalogue printed in an edition of 1,200 copies by Specialblue, London.

Printed in the UK

ISBN 0 947912 18 5

**Lothian Hospital
Arts Consortium**

Cover Photo: Bangour Village Hospital Grounds, Kate Gray 2001